POLITICS

Eduard Altarriba

BUTTON BOOKS

“Man is by nature a political animal”

Aristotle, *Politics*, Book 1, 1253a.

Contents

The world's first societies were small, with few people. This meant everyone knew everyone else and knew who was in charge (who had power). But as they grew, some villages gained influence over others and the first civilizations emerged. These were societies made up of several villages, and it was no longer possible for people to know everyone. There were a few people who told others what to do, and everyone else did what they were told. How were these complex societies organized?

POWER

is the ability some people have to influence others.

A person with power can be in charge, give orders, make decisions, or make others with less (or no) power do or not do things.

Parents have power over their children.

A boss has power over the workers.

A general gives orders to their officers.

A prestigious intellectual can influence the decisions of others.

The police are in charge of keeping order in society.

A government creates laws for people to follow.

In all societies, from the smallest to the largest, **power is shared out**.

Some people have a lot of power, others have little, and many have hardly any.

Each society (such as tribes, cities, and countries) organizes power differently.

People want to have the power to organize their society in the way they think best, according to their ideology and interests.

Power comes with huge responsibility, as many people depend on the decisions that are taken.

But power also brings prestige and privilege. Also, whoever has power gets to decide how resources and wealth are shared out.

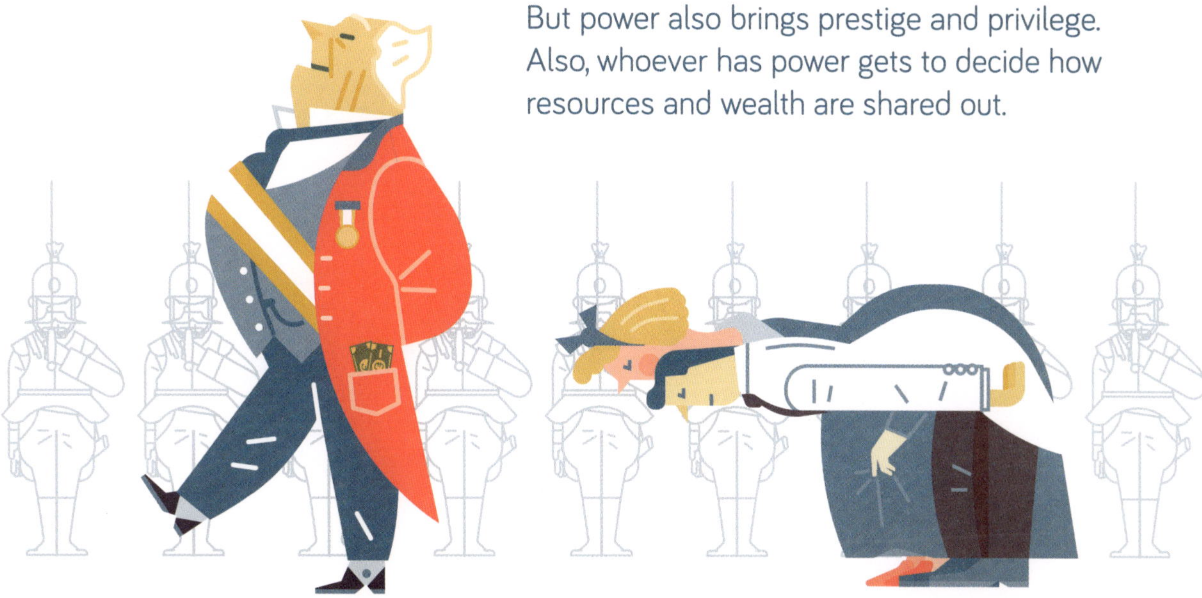

In any society, there are many people and groups **competing for power**. This competition can lead to **POLITICAL CONFLICT**.

Social hierarchies

A king is not the same as a mayor or a delivery person. The king has much more power than a mayor and the mayor has more power than a delivery person. But there are very few kings, lots of mayors, and even more delivery people.

Power often works like a pyramid: toward the top, it is concentrated in the hands of a few people. Toward the bottom, power is diluted among more people, giving them less ability to organize and influence things. In democracies, it works this way too. You can vote for the politicians but not change the economic and political system.

Between the top and the bottom, there are several intermediate levels, and between all levels there is a HIERARCHICAL RELATIONSHIP, in other words, a power relationship where those at the top have greater authority than those at the bottom.

In traditional societies, it was very hard to move from one class to another, but in modern societies, although it is not always easy, it is possible.

Elites

POWER has a lot to do with how wealth is distributed within a society: nearly always, the richest people are the ones who have the most power and influence over the people who govern (if the rich people are not governing directly themselves).

The groups at the very top are called elites. They are not only the richest and most powerful people, but in most cases they also have social prestige, education, knowledge, and information.

The different groups are constantly fighting to gain and/or to keep power.

Middle class

People who are in the middle class have more power and wealth than the working class but less than the elites. Members of the middle class often have jobs that require a university degree, but will probably need to borrow money to buy a house or a new car.

Working class

The working class try to improve their situation (or at least make sure it doesn't get worse). As there are many of them, if they all decide to disobey or attack the center of power at the same time, they can bring about change.

For example, the world's richest people tend to study at the most prestigious universities, such as Harvard (USA) or Cambridge (UK), where they mix with other people in the same social class. Thanks to their studies and their contacts, when they finish university they will go into top jobs.

The different levels of the pyramid represent the different social classes with their different interests.

In the animal kingdom, we can find many examples of small communities where the strongest rules. Brute force is the most primal form of power.

Humans can also use force to gain power, although in a more organized and complex way.

VIOLENCE!

Violence, or the fear of violence, has always been one of the most effective ways to gain power. But violence is also used to challenge power.

THE LAW OF THE STRONGEST

When a person or a group is very strong, it is easy for them to gain power by using violence. But once they are in power, there is always a danger that another even stronger group might take it away from them.

ORDER AND DEFENSE

Nearly all political systems have armies and police to maintain law and order in society. But these are also used to defend the country against external and internal threats.

During the Middle Ages in Europe, power was in the hands of feudal lords who controlled small territories and were at war among themselves. To protect themselves from the violence, peasants agreed to be ruled by a lord who offered them protection. In exchange, the peasants had to pay taxes to the lord and sometimes they were treated like slaves.

WARS

Throughout history, humans living in tribes, kingdoms, empires, republics, and states have fought each other to stay in power or gain more power, resources, and wealth.

The great empires in history, such as the Roman Empire, the Ming Dynasty in China, and the British colonial empire have all been based on military conquest.

Violence and war have always been a quick way to gain power, whether by conquering a country, overthrowing a government, or changing a whole society with a revolution.

Sadly, states today continue to use war to defend or impose their interests.

Having power is not the same as

GOVERNING

There are some very powerful people who do not govern. For example, an executive of a multinational company or a senior military commander can give orders to thousands of people, but they don't govern a country or a region. There have even been kings who, although they had absolute power, left government matters in the hands of their ministers.

GOVERNING means directing and administering the public affairs of a society or community.

This can mean governing a country, empire, region, city, town, neighborhood, or even a university or international organization.

ADMINISTERING means making sure that all the things a government controls, from hospitals to prisons, work properly. There are many people who work for the state, called civil servants, who look after the day-to-day running of the public sector (services for the population): teachers, police, tax collectors, health workers, and more.

Laws and regulations

Just like the rules that say what you can and cannot do in a game of soccer, all societies have rules, regulations, and laws that cover rights, responsibilities, and things that are not allowed. These rules change from one society to another as most people have to agree to them, so they are based on history, traditions, and different political approaches (which often change).

One of the first known sets of written laws is the Code of Hammurabi, composed in 1754 BCE by the Babylonian king, Hammurabi. Over 200 laws were written on a stone stele. They cover matters such as property, trade, crime, contracts, marriage, and the penalties that apply to those who do not obey.

POLITICAL THOUGHT

Politics is the way that power is organized within a society, how decisions that affect everyone are taken, and how resources are shared out. But **what is the best way to do this?**

Since ancient times, in places as different as Greece, China, and India, some people began to ask themselves what was the best way to govern a society.

Athens became one of the most important cities in Ancient Greece. At its peak, it had a democratic system: the men who had the right to vote met in assemblies to discuss and vote on matters relating to the governing of the city.

In contrast, Athens' rival, Sparta, was governed by a small group of the city's aristocratic elite. And over the sea, an all-powerful king reigned over the Persian Empire, the Greeks' great enemy.

The word "democracy" comes from the Greek words **δήμος** ("people") and **κρατώ** ("power"): THE POWER OF THE PEOPLE

In Ancient Greece, only men from particular social groups could take part in the assemblies. Women, enslaved people, and foreigners were all excluded.

In other words, most of the population was not allowed to take part in the political life of the society.

What is the best form of government?

A government is a system used to govern a state. Governments and rulers should make policies that benefit the whole of society (or at least as many people as possible). But sometimes policies only really benefit the rulers and the elites who support them.

In these cases, we can say it is a CORRUPT GOVERNMENT. The most corrupt governments tend to be AUTHORITARIAN: they use fear and violence to stay in power (although corruption can be found in other forms of government).

Aristotle was one of the first thinkers who wrote about the best way to govern a society.

ONE-MAN RULE

For Aristotle, **MONARCHY** was government by one virtuous man (few women reigned back then). But if the king was corrupted by power, he became a **TYRANT**: a man who reigns for his own benefit and uses fear and violence.

GOVERNMENT OF THE FEW

A group of virtuous and just people can rule wisely. Aristotle called this form of government **ARISTOCRACY**. But if that group rule for their own benefit, it becomes an **OLIGARCHY**: government by a few rich, corrupt men.

GOVERNMENT OF THE MANY

A government where most of the population participates in group decisions is called a **DEMOCRACY**. Aristotle did not trust the ability of the masses to understand and decide on matters of government. He thought that someone intelligent and with good public speaking skills might manipulate the assemblies.

Confucious (China, 6th century BCE) thought that society should be governed by a virtuous and exemplary monarch. Helped by wise counselors, he would be like a father to his subjects and maintain order and tradition.

Jean-Jaques Rousseau (Europe, 1712–1778) argued that human beings are good by nature, but that life in society exposes them to inequalities and rules that corrupt them. He therefore put forward the idea of a "social contract" between individuals and the community that would guarantee the equality and freedom of all citizens. These ideas influenced the development of modern democratic thought.

Maintaining power through fear and violence alone is very complicated. The people in power need to maintain permanent control over most of the population.

The best way to stop people from challenging those in power is to make sure that they accept their leader's right to lead and are even willing to defend it.

LEGITIMACY

Legitimacy is the acceptance of authority, of whoever is in charge.

People accept the right of a person to lead for many reasons. It may be because of the leader's prestige, leadership style, religious beliefs, customs and traditions, tribal ties, or political ideologies (or a combination of several of these factors).

There is also a whole body of thought about the legitimacy of power that looks at obedience, loyalty, the sense of duty, belonging to a group, allegiance, and religion. These are all things that can help a society to come together around a political system.

There is a whole set of symbols associated with power: crowns, flags, emblems, ceremonies, national anthems, and so on.

In medieval European monarchies, the right to rule was HEREDITARY. This meant the crown passed from father to son by custom and tradition, and in some cases because people believed it was God's will. Allegiance to the king, the nobility, and the church was one of the fundamental values of these political regimes.

PEACE AND ORDER

Conflict, violence, and war make life unsafe and dangerous.

People prefer to live in peace to work, trade, raise their children, and celebrate their festivals and rituals.

That is why most people want a political system that guarantees their safety and security. And even if they don't agree with the government, they prefer to use peaceful ways to express their disagreement so that peace is guaranteed.

There are various ways to maintain social order:

Exercise such strong power that it is too scary to oppose it, therefore imposing peace (as in dictatorships and absolute monarchies).

With very strong bonds in societies where people have very similar backgrounds, such as a tribe or some religious societies.

Establish and apply rules and laws through politics and justice, as in modern democracies.

Societies are often a combination of these different things.

THE STATE

The idea of the state as we know it, meaning a group of people occupying a particular territory, became established around the 19th century. Today, the world is divided into states. Most of these refer to themselves as democracies.

International recognition

To establish diplomatic relations, states need to be part of international organizations such as the United Nations (UN) and sign treaties with other states.

Public administration

This includes institutions, offices, and a body of civil servants that allow the government to function and have a relationship with its citizens.

Political institutions

The state has institutions such as a parliament, a judicial system that applies the law, and an executive that governs the country (see page 28).

Centralized governments

These generally have the most important institutions in the country's **capital** even though they govern the entire national territory.

See centralized and federal states, p.34

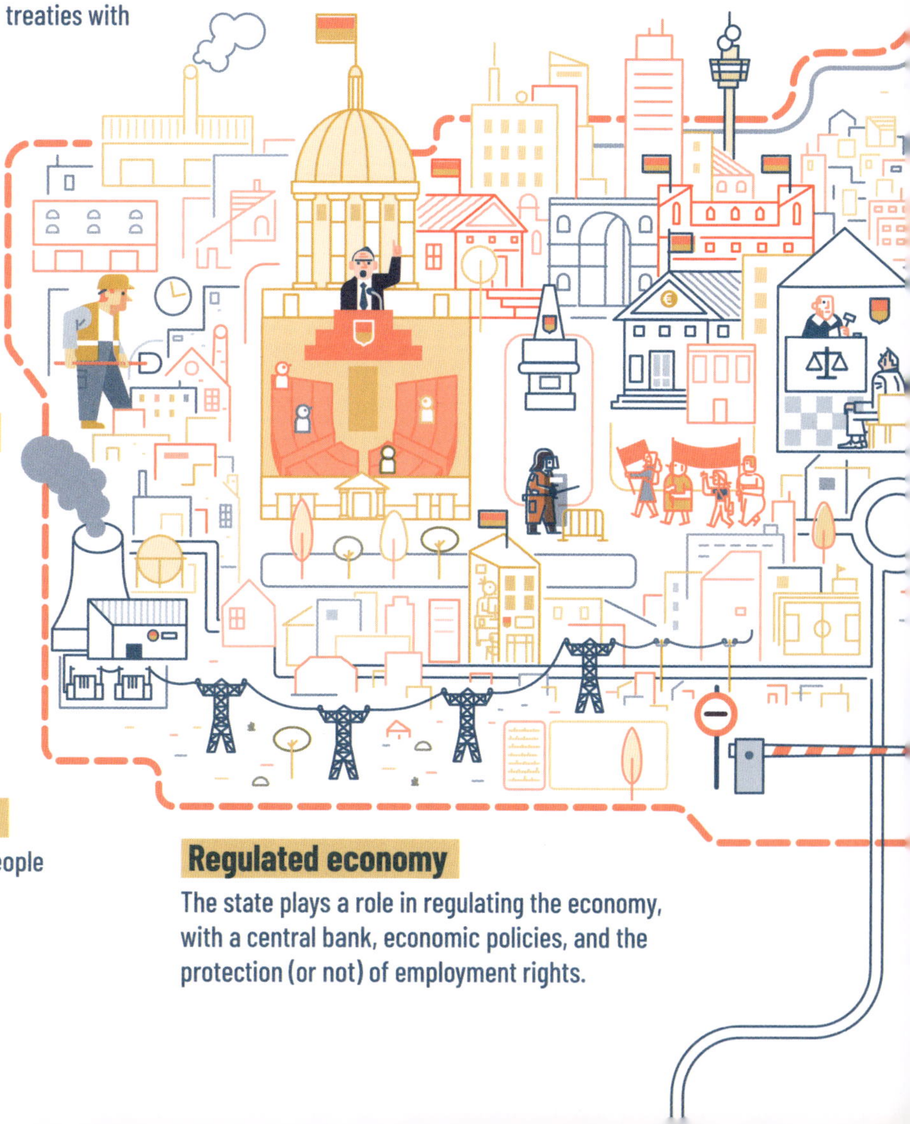

Taxes and public finances

The state collects taxes from the people to pay for its activities and provide public services such as education, health, and security.

Regulated economy

The state plays a role in regulating the economy, with a central bank, economic policies, and the protection (or not) of employment rights.

National symbols

States have a flag, a national anthem, one or more languages, and a shared culture and history.

TERRITORY AND SOVEREIGNTY

A state has a territory that is defined by its borders.

And it has the right and duty to take decisions and create laws within its borders.

CITIZENSHIP

Citizenship is the legal recognition of belonging to a state. This gives people certain **rights** (such as voting and having a passport) and **duties** (such as paying taxes).

Army

Countries have armed forces to defend themselves and their interests.

Law and order

The state has a legal system which passes and applies laws. Judges, police, and civil servants make sure that the laws are respected.

Monopoly of force

Only the state has the right to use force and violence (within legal limits) to maintain order and security.

The police and the military are the main state bodies that can use force.

Infrastructure

The state (often in partnership with private companies) builds airports, dams, roads, hospitals, and everything else that is needed for the country's economy to function.

THE ECONOMY

All societies have a system for producing and sharing out goods and wealth. The different ways of doing this generate different economic and political systems:

Economic liberalism

According to this theory, the state **doesn't interfere in the economy** because the economy is assumed to be self-regulating. People are free to earn money and own private property. The state's role is therefore limited to guaranteeing free trade (where states allow goods and services to be imported and exported with little or no taxes), security, and private property.

Planned economy

According to this theory, the state must have **total control over the economy** to ensure equality and to share out wealth fairly. Most companies are state-owned and the authorities decide which goods to produce, which services to provide, quantities, prices, and so on.

Mixed economy

This sits midway between liberalism and a planned economy. It **guarantees a free market** (where the government doesn't seek to control the economy) **and private property**, however, **some companies are owned by the state and the government collects taxes, makes decisions about the economy, and guarantees rights, services, and protection to its citizens**.

Many states have opted for a mixed economy and a democratic political system. These are called LIBERAL DEMOCRACIES.

States need a lot of money to function. Governments therefore collect

TAXES

People and companies pay taxes to the state.

Paying taxes is compulsory.

The state has institutions in charge of collecting taxes.

The money the state collects is returned to the nation in various ways that help the economy and the population:

- Paying civil servants (such as teachers, police, diplomats, and tax inspectors).
- Paying pensions to retired people.
- Building infrastructure such as hospitals, airports, schools, and roads.
- Funding academic and scientific research and development.
- Paying for many other things.

STATE BUDGET

This is the document the government draws up every year to set out its planned spending: when, how much, and on what the money will be spent.

BORDERS AND SECURITY

States have defined borders. Within these borders, the government has the power to carry out its laws and policies.

Police, customs officials, and the army control the borders and monitor the entry and exit of people and goods.* The state sets the conditions for people to enter its territory and imposes taxes for certain goods.

International border

Embassies (see below) are outside the control of the country where they are located. For example, the French police cannot enter the UK embassy in Paris without permission from the UK.

DIPLOMACY

States can establish diplomatic relations with each other. This includes countries being able to open embassies and consulates in other countries. From these offices, ambassadors and other diplomats represent their country's interests abroad, promote its culture, help its citizens, negotiate treaties, and work to prevent conflicts.

*In Europe's Schengen area, there is free movement of people and goods.

ARMED FORCES

The armed forces have various functions, such as defending the national territory, assisting other countries when they are facing a crisis, and defending the state's interests abroad. But they can also be used to repress the population, overthrow the government, or attack other countries.

POLICE

The police force is responsible for maintaining order and making sure the law is followed.

It works with police forces in other countries to fight against terrorism and international gangs.

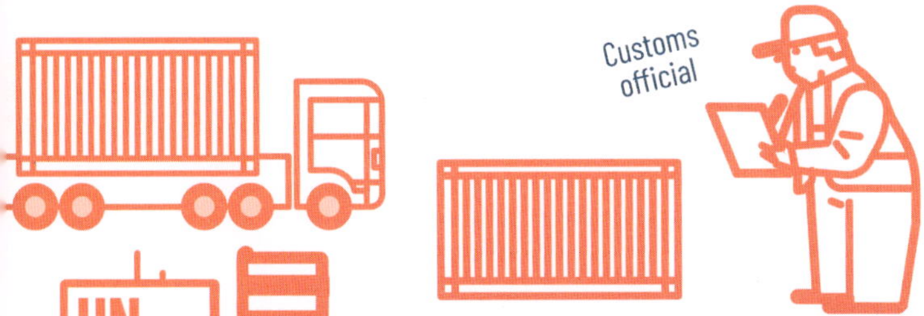

FOREIGN POLICY

Foreign policy is the way a country maintains relationships with other countries. This might include economic agreements, military partnerships, managing migration, cultural exchanges, or combating international crime.

INTELLIGENCE SERVICES

Governments have agencies that work in secret to gather and analyze information to detect threats to national and international security.

But they can also be used to spy on governments or foreign companies or to prevent other countries from spying on them.

Sometimes they are used to keep watch on and control political groups that are opposed to the government or the economic system.

MONARCHIES AND REPUBLICS

In the Middle Ages (from about 500 to 1500 CE), most territories were organized around the figure of the monarch (or tsar, prince, emperor, basileus, or some other name). Today, monarchies still exist but most no longer have the power they had centuries ago.

CONSTITUTIONAL MONARCHIES

This is the most common type of monarchy in Europe. People do not vote for a monarch—it is a hereditary position.

The monarch's function is defined in each country's law and constitution. The monarch reigns but does not govern or form part of the state government.

The monarch is the head of state. He or she has a ceremonial role and is a symbol of the country.

Examples: the United Kingdom, Belgium, Spain, Japan, and Tonga.

ABSOLUTE MONARCHIES

In this model of the state, the monarch and his or her family either still hold all the power and rule the country or have a lot of power over the government.

This is the model in Qatar, Saudi Arabia, and the United Arab Emirates.

In other countries, the monarch has some limited functions within the constitution, but still has some power that he or she shares with the government.

This is the case in Morocco, Thailand, Jordan, and Monaco.

When states do not have a monarch, they are called **REPUBLICS**. All this means is that they have no monarch. They can have a liberal, socialist, authoritarian, or any other kind of political system.

Most countries in the world are republics, for example, France, the United States, the Russian Federation, Brazil, and India.

I'M IN CHARGE HERE!

The military and the police often play a key role in dictatorships. Dictators are sometimes military men or have the support of the military.

DICTATORSHIPS are political regimes in which power is concentrated in the hands of just one person or an oligarchy (a small group of people). Dictators exercise power for their personal benefit or that of their social group. To gain and maintain power, they often use violence and repression against a large part of the population that does not have any guaranteed rights or freedom.

Some authoritarian states are republics where the head of state can have as much or more power than an absolutist monarch. They can even make their role hereditary!

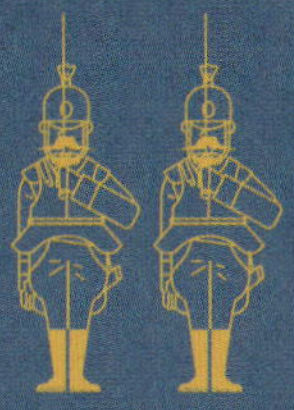

AUTHORITARIAN STATES can claim that they are democratic, but in fact they have policies that tend to be more typical of a dictatorship, such as no freedom of the press, no freedom of expression, persecuting people for their political opinions, and little separation of powers (see page 28).

(REPRESENTATIVE) DEMOCRACY

CITIZENS* (people with citizenship) with a right to vote can take part in democratic elections.

*Children and foreigners who do not have citizenship cannot vote. People may also be barred from voting for other reasons, such as if they are in prison or have been convicted of an electoral offence.

LEGITIMACY

In order to be considered democratic, elections have to meet certain requirements to make sure they are fair and represent the will of the people. For their part, the representatives have to respect the separation of powers (see page 28) and the law. The legitimacy of democracies depends on this.

The **DECISIONS** taken by the representatives, the laws they pass, and the way they govern affects everyone.

TYPES OF DEMOCRACY

Direct or participatory democracy:
Citizens have greater decision-making power over government matters. They take part in assemblies, referendums, and open forums.

Representative democracy:
Citizens elect their representatives, who are the ones that take decisions. This is the most common form of democracy.

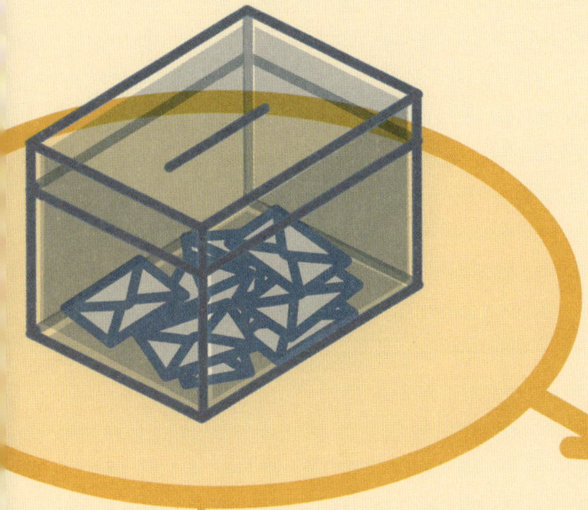

People with the right to vote, vote in official **ELECTIONS** (national, regional, local, etc.)

These elections return elected **REPRESENTATIVES** from different political parties.

The representatives use the state's institutions and structures to **GOVERN**.

SEPARATION OF POWERS

Most democratic states are split into three branches. In the most advanced type of democracy, these can make decisions and work independently.

LEGISLATIVE POWER

Passes laws used by the state to govern and keeps executive power in check.

PARLIAMENT

JUDICIAL POWER

Interprets and applies laws passe by the legislature, impartially and fairly in the event of conflict.

JUDGES AND MAGISTRATES

EXECUTIVE POWER

Applies laws and public policies passed by the legislature, manages the day-to-day running of the state, and makes administrative decisions.

HEAD OF GOVERNMENT

MINISTERS

HEAD OF STATE

Parliament is the place where elected members put forward, debate, and pass laws and public policies.

One of the basic principles of most democracies is the division of power. This stops too much power from being concentrated in the hands of one person or group.

The separation of powers is fundamental in a state governed by the rule of law (see page 31). Its is to guarantee the proper functioning of the government and institutions, guarantee rights and freedoms, and avoid a drift toward authoritarianism.

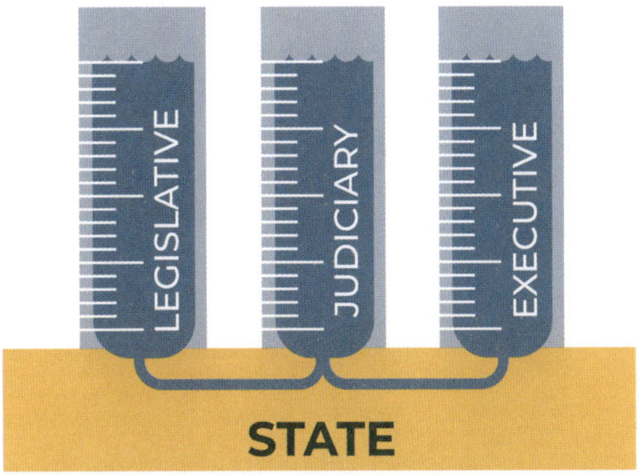

In representative democracies, the three branches must coordinate and counterbalance each other for the state to function properly.

For example, in a democracy, the president or prime minster cannot order judges to convict a political opponent. In the same way, judges cannot tell parliament or the government which laws to pass.

Members of the government take important decisions on policies and state matters.

They also propose laws to parliament.

Ministers are in charge of a particular area of government, such as health, the economy, defense, or education.

Although the three branches are independent, states have different systems of checks and balances between the different branches.

THE CONSTITUTION

When a state adopts a political system, such as a democracy, it defines its structure, the way it functions, and the rights and duties of both the government and citizens. All of this is recorded in the constitution.

Most of the world's constitutions were written in the 19th and 20th centuries.

All the laws that a country makes must follow the principles of the constitution.

For example, if the constitution says that you cannot apply the death penalty, no law must include the death penalty.

Constitutions are usually written in one document, but they can also be made up of different documents, as is the case in the United Kingdom.

CAN CONSTITUTIONS BE CHANGED?

Yes, but as they are the foundation for the political and social system, only small changes or amendments can be made. Some countries do this frequently, while the constitutions in other countries have not been touched since they were signed. But if a country wants to change its entire political and legal system, a new constitution must be drawn up and approved.

RULE OF LAW

In a state governed by the rule of law, the law is considered to be more important than everything else. A state governed by the rule of law must follow certain principles: the division of power, universal access to justice, equality before the law, and respect for fundamental rights and individual freedoms.

THE CONSTITUTIONAL COURT* is responsible for checking that all laws and actions taken by the government do not contradict what the constitution says.

* The name and functions of the court vary from country to the country.

FUNDAMENTAL RIGHTS

These are the rights and freedoms that all people have. They are the basis of a modern democratic state (and its constitution).

Civil rights

Freedom of expression
Religious freedom
Freedom of assembly and association
Right to privacy
Etc.

Political rights

Right to vote
Right to political participation
Protection against discrimination
Right to stand as a candidate
Etc.

Social and economic rights

Right to education
Right to work
Right to housing
Etc.

Judicial and legal rights

Right to be presumed innocent
Right to legal defense
Environmental rights
Etc.

You can find more information about fundamental rights on https://www.un.org/en/about-us/universal-declaration-of-human-rights

Public policies

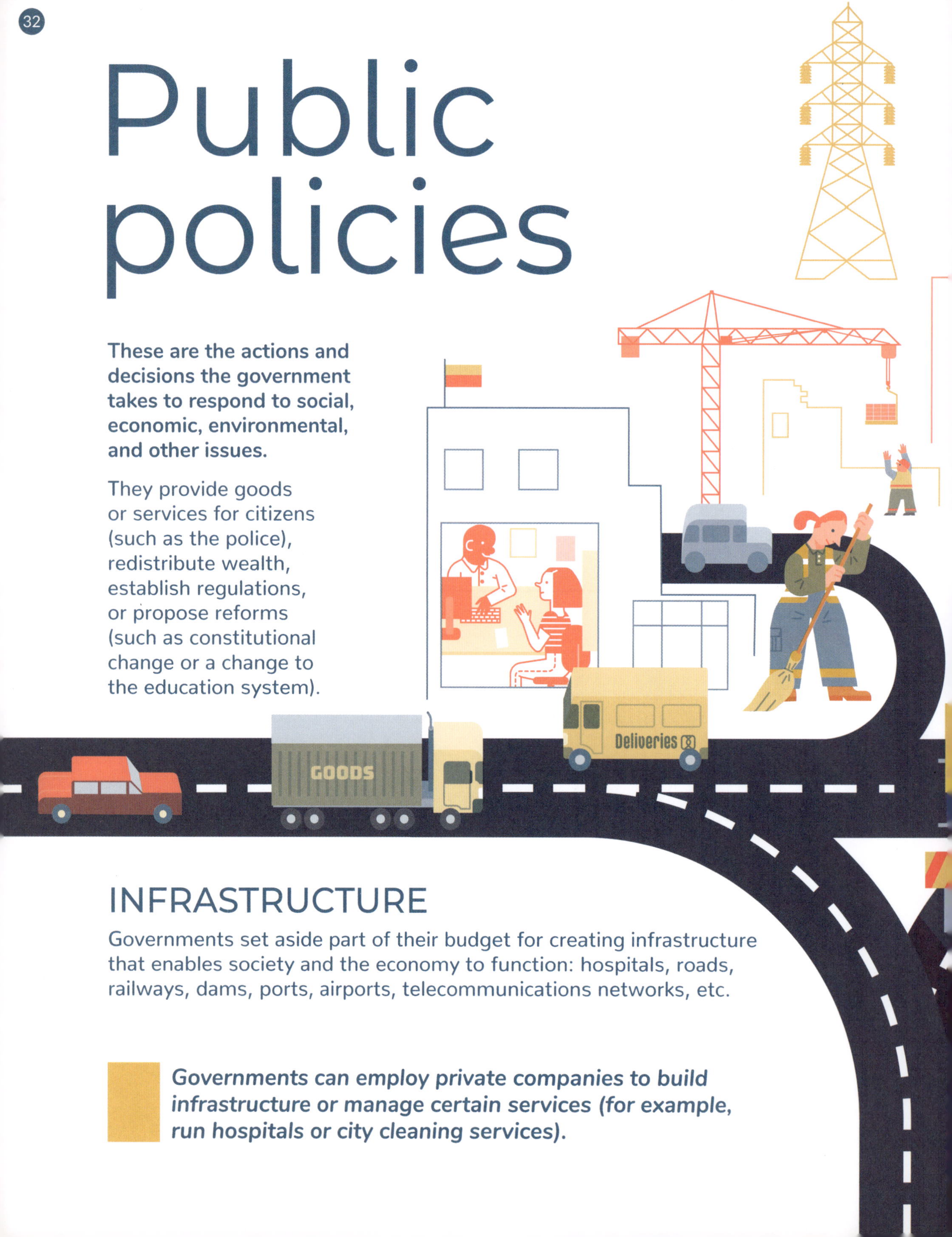

These are the actions and decisions the government takes to respond to social, economic, environmental, and other issues.

They provide goods or services for citizens (such as the police), redistribute wealth, establish regulations, or propose reforms (such as constitutional change or a change to the education system).

INFRASTRUCTURE

Governments set aside part of their budget for creating infrastructure that enables society and the economy to function: hospitals, roads, railways, dams, ports, airports, telecommunications networks, etc.

Governments can employ private companies to build infrastructure or manage certain services (for example, run hospitals or city cleaning services).

PUBLIC/PRIVATE

There is a difference between what is public (belongs to the state and therefore the people) and private (belongs to one or more individuals).

Privately owned companies are owned by business people or shareholders. Their aim is financial profit. They have the right to operate within established legal limits.

Publicly owned companies are owned by the state. Their purpose is to provide goods or services that are essential to everyone. They operate like a normal company, but they belong to everyone in the country.

When a public administration, such as a city council, is not able to provide a certain service, it can employ a private company to do so. This is an **outsourced service**.

There are also ***joint ventures*** *that are funded partly by the state and partly by private companies.*

Workers from a private company building a public road.

PRIVATIZATION

From the point of view of economic liberalism (see page 20), public companies are considered inefficient and a big expense for the state (making taxes too high as a result).

This is why some governments choose to sell public companies to private investors. In other words, public companies become private companies. This is called privatization.

Public administration is all the organization needed for the state to put its public policies into practice.

Although states have a central government, the administration has different levels, branches, and geographical locations with different powers.

For example, the town or city council can make regulations on the maximum height of apartment blocks in its district, but it cannot open embassies in other countries.

However, the central government can open embassies in other countries and create regulations that affect the whole country. But it does not make regulations on the height of apartment blocks in a particular city.

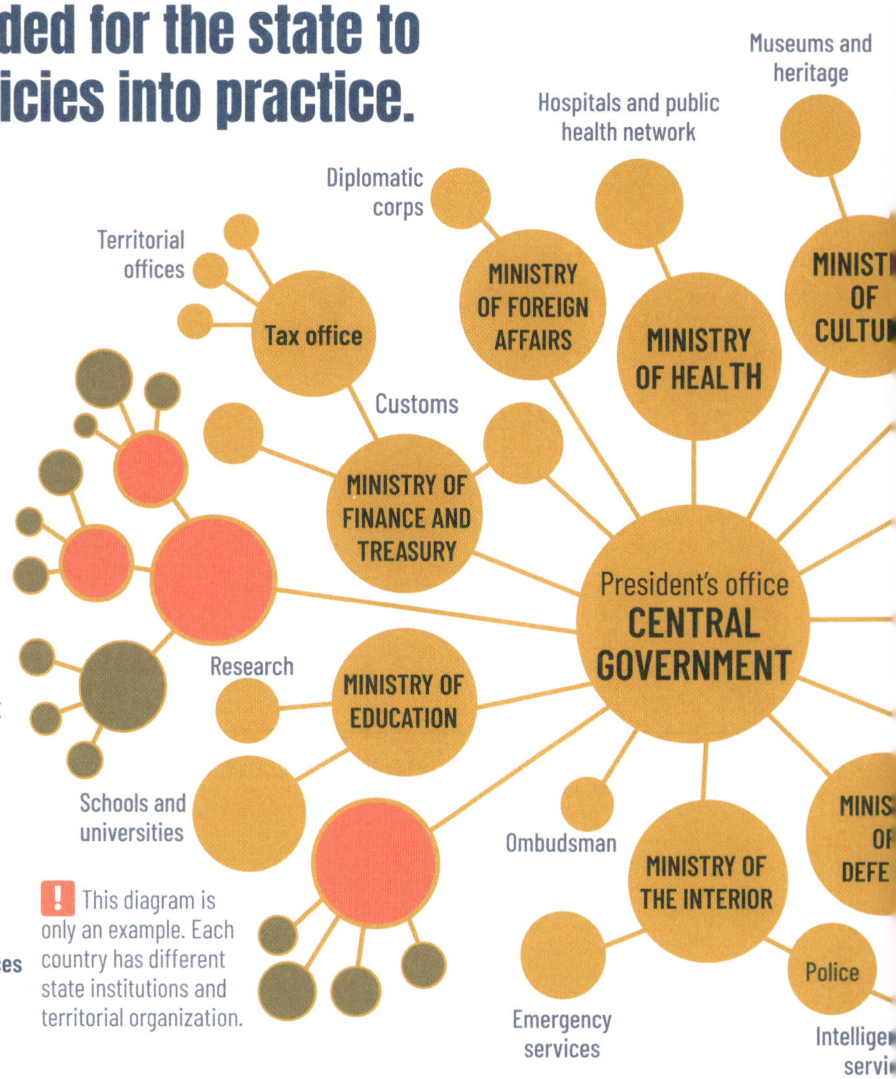

CENTRAL GOVERNMENT

Governments and/or territorial offices

City councils and local government

! This diagram is only an example. Each country has different state institutions and territorial organization.

CENTRALIZED/FEDERAL STATE

There are countries where the central government has most of the legislative power of the state. These are **CENTRALIZED** states and are the most common model.

In other countries, regions or states keep a large part of the legislative capacity, while the central government is in charge of some areas such as defense, economic policy, or foreign policy. These are **FEDERAL STATES**.

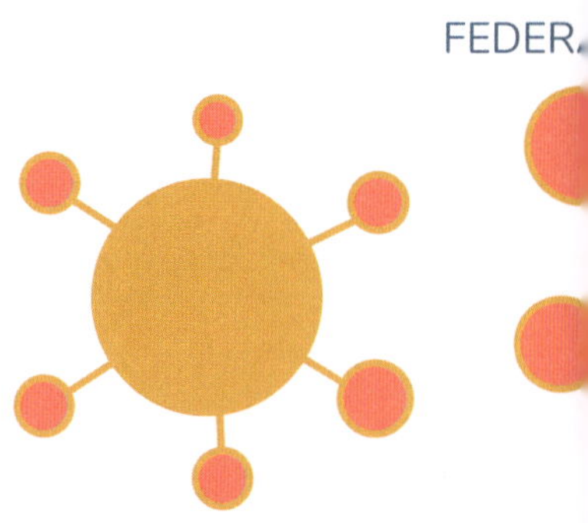

Some geographical regions might be autonomous, meaning they have the power to make their own decisions in some areas, such as education, health, and culture.

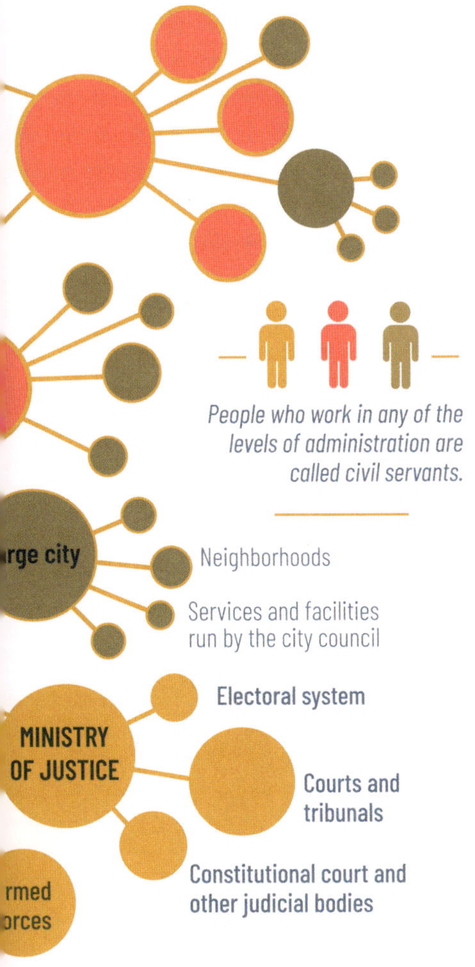

People who work in any of the levels of administration are called civil servants.

Examples of centralized states are France and Turkey.

Examples of federal states are Germany and the USA.

Countries such as Spain are partway between the two models.

ENTITIES ABOVE STATES

Some countries have grouped together in supranational organizations (entities above states) to work together on issues that go beyond their borders.

To join these supranational groups, states have to fulfill certain requirements that may require giving up part of their sovereignty. Here are some examples:

UN (United Nations)

This is an organization created after the Second World War to promote world peace and help to resolve international conflicts. It is currently made up of 193 countries.*

NATO (North Atlantic Treaty Organization)

This is the military alliance led by the USA, bringing together mainly European and North American countries. Although its role is defensive (if a NATO country is attacked, all other NATO members have to defend it), it is also a tool for political and international pressure. It is currently made up of 32 countries.*

EU (European Union)

This started out as an economic union, but it has become the political and economic power that brings together a majority of European countries. It has legislative, executive, and judicial powers over member countries. Most member states are democratic countries with mixed economies (see page 20) and nearly all use the euro as their currency. It is currently made up of 27 countries.*

*Data as of April 2024

VOTE!

Elections are the way citizens elect their representatives (rulers). Citizens vote to express their political preferences and decide who will hold public office and take decisions on their behalf.

Who runs for election?

In theory, in a democracy any adult citizen has the right to stand for election and be elected as a political representative.

In practice, however, they need an infrastructure, people working for them, and a lot of money to run in elections (especially national ones). This favors the **big political parties** that can present candidates and run big campaigns. Political parties are organizations of people who share similar views on how their country should be run (see page 38).

Electoral laws in each country define how elections are run.

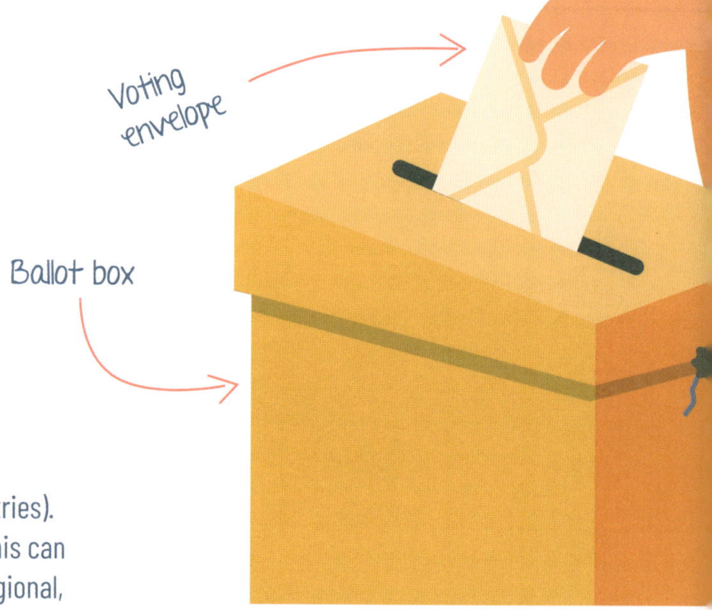

Who can vote in elections?

All **citizens** who are adults (18 years old in most countries). The electoral roll is the list of people who can vote. This can vary depending on whether the elections are local, regional, national, or supranational. In national or supranational elections, the whole country votes. In regional elections, only people in that particular region or state vote, and in local elections, only people in that town or city vote.

! *The election timeline on the opposite page is just an example, and the actual timeline will depend on the electoral system and the type of election.*

The vote is secret. This is why sealed envelopes or folded voting slips are put in sealed ballot boxes. Voting can also be done electronically or by post.

TIMELINE OF AN ELECTION

1 ELECTION IS CALLED

Elections take place at specific intervals of time (for example, every four years), but sometimes they happen sooner because of a political crisis. When an election is called, the exact day of voting is given.

Based on this, the candidates start preparing and the electoral campaign starts. Most candidates represent political parties.

2 ELECTORAL CAMPAIGN

During electoral campaigns, political parties or candidates explain their proposals and electoral manifestos so that people can consider whether to vote for them. They organize rallies, public events, and various campaign activities such as posters in the streets, adverts on television, social media, and debates.

During this period **POLLS** are taken and published so everyone can see who people are planning to vote for.

3 VOTING

People go to **POLLING STATIONS** to vote. These are places like schools or conference halls that are used for voting on that day.

4 COUNT

When the polling stations close, the vote count starts. It can go on for hours or even days, depending on the number of votes and the system used.

5 RESULTS

Once all the votes are counted, the official results are announced publicly. These tell us which parties and candidates have won the most votes.

In electoral systems with two rounds, the whole process is repeated a second time if no candidate has won an overall majority (see page 40) in the first round.

FROM LEFT

FAR LEFT | LEFT | CENTER-LEFT

Progressive or left-wing political parties

These parties believe that the government should protect the most disadvantaged people in society and guarantee basic services (such as health and education), equality, diversity, and the fundamental rights of the population. In order to achieve this, they believe in greater state involvement in the economy, collecting higher taxes (especially from the wealthiest classes), and prioritizing social policies.

POLITICAL PARTIES

These are organizations of people that group together around a political ideology and want to govern or influence policies.

Within parties, there are usually **FACTIONS**—different opposing groups that compete to control the party and its ideology.

The **LEADER** is the most powerful person in the party. She or he is usually the visible face in campaigns and in the media. She or he may or may not also be the candidate for president.

TO RIGHT

Political parties traditionally sit somewhere on the Left to Right (or Progressive to Conservative) scale.

CENTER-RIGHT | RIGHT | FAR RIGHT

n many countries, nost voters vote or center-right or center-left candidates.

Conservative or right-wing political parties

These parties tend to support the traditional social order and private property. They prioritize individual rights, security, and public order. They believe the state should invest less in social services and they favor private companies through lower taxation and less regulation.

Besides right and left, parties may have different positions on particular issues (regional, religious, nationalist, and so on).

For example, a right-wing party might be strongly against immigration, while another right-wing or center-right party might think that controlled immigration is necessary for the economy.

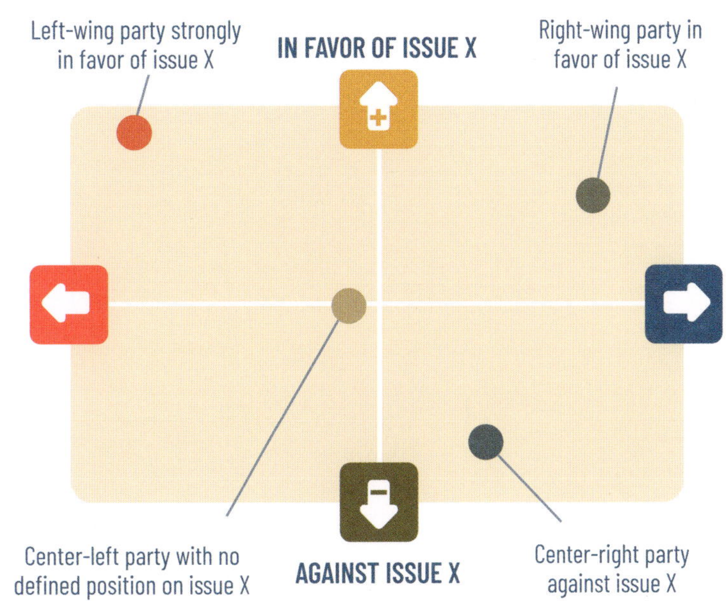

MAJORITIES AND COALITIONS

In non-presidential parliamentary systems, the prime minister or president is elected by a vote by the elected members of the parliament. This is why they need to win a majority, in other words, more than half of the votes.

If the party that has won the election has a big enough majority, it can vote for the president and form a government without a problem.

But if it does not have this majority, it has to form pacts called **coalitions** with other parties, so that they either vote for its candidate or abstain.*

*If a party abstains (does not vote yes or no), the number of votes needed to get a majority changes.

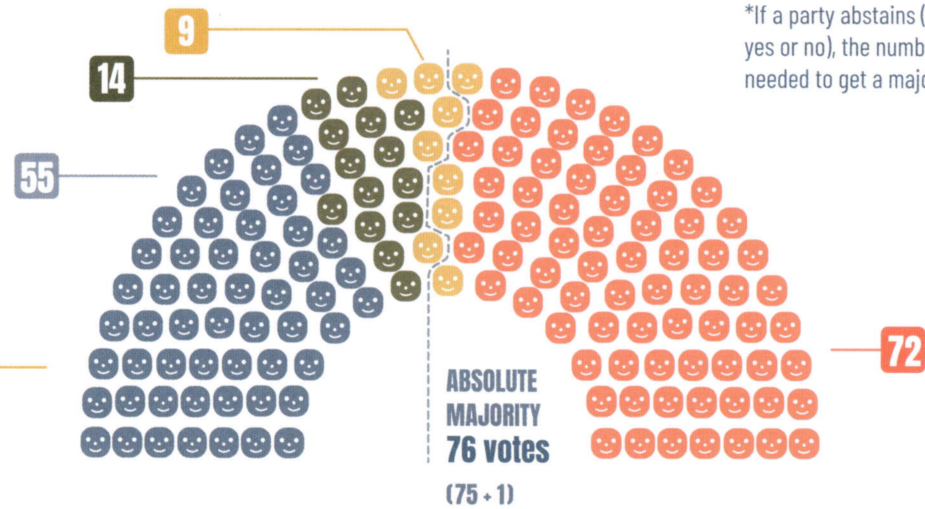

Imagine a parliament with seats for **150 members of parliament** (or deputies).

After the election, these are the results:

- The RED party has won **72 seats**
- The YELLOW party has won **9 seats**
- The GREEN party has won **14 seats**
- The BLUE party has won **55 seats**

A majority requires more than half of the 150 seats—in other words, 76 seats.

The REDS have won, but they are four seats short of the 76 needed to vote for the president they want.

They could make a pact with the YELLOWS to get a majority.

72 + 9 = 81

Or they could make a pact with the GREENS and get an even bigger majority.

72 + 14 = 86

But the BLUES could also make a pact with the YELLOWS and the GREENS to get a majority if the REDS can't make their own pact. They could then govern as a coalition and vote for another president, even though they did not win the elections.

55 + 9 + 14 = 78

In this situation, the party that won the election is not going to govern.

WHO ARE THE HIGHEST AUTHORITIES IN A COUNTRY?

HEAD OF GOVERNMENT

HEAD OF STATE

Leader of the executive	**The country's representative**
This is the leader of the executive branch. They are in charge of running the government and implementing policies and laws. Some examples of heads of government are presidents (Spain), prime ministers (United Kingdom), and chancellors (Germany and Austria).	The head of state's duties can be mainly symbolic and ceremonial, as in constitutional monarchies (for example, the United Kingdom and Spain). But they can also have some executive powers and control over the government, as in the case with some presidents (for example, France).

Duties and power can vary depending on the country and the political system.

These responsibilities can be held by one person (for example, the president in the USA), by two different people (for example, the prime minister and the king in the United Kingdom), or even be shared between a group of people.

THE POLITICAL ARENA

Politics is not just done from within political parties and government institutions. There are many people (or "actors") who take part in politics and put forward their opinions, support causes, and promote their group's interests.

The more people and opinions there are in the political arena, the more points of view the government will have to take into account when making policies.

The government will also have to give more explanation about the decisions it makes and will be more closely monitored.

COMPANIES

These **people and organizations** try to directly **influence policies** in different ways: through campaigns, lobbying (trying to influence the decisions of government), demonstrating, or running as candidates in elections.

Within this group of actors, there are social movements, organizations that **promote social change**, and pressure groups or companies that **lobby** for their own **economic and business interests**.

LOBBYISTS

MEDIA

RELIGIOUS GROUPS

FREEDOM OF THE PRESS AND FREEDOM OF EXPRESSION

In a democracy, everyone should be able to say what they think and all political sides should have the right to publicly express their ideas and proposals.

Similarly, people also have the right to listen to all the ideas and opinions in order to be well-informed and vote for the candidate they think best.

These principles also mean that people working in the media and the arts (books, movies, theater, etc.) should be able to express themselves freely and criticize those that have economic or political power without fear of censorship or reprisals.

PROPAGANDA

Political communication (from political parties, labor unions, and others) is an attempt to connect with voters to influence their behavior and opinions.

PUBLIC OPINION is what the people in general think about a particular issue.

So we could say, for example, that public opinion is for or against protecting the environment, or that public opinion is divided on tax reforms.

The POLITICAL AGENDA is made up of current issues and problems as public opinion sees it.

One of the communication strategies of political parties is to try to steer this agenda by choosing the issues that best fit into their ideology. That way, they can appear in the media and reinforce their message. They also choose issues that will get them the most votes.

The more visibility the political parties have in the traditional media (television, radio, etc.) and on social media, the more influence they have. This is why they use simple and effective messages to generate headlines and attract the attention of the public.

Communication campaigns are at their busiest during elections.

AND COMMUNICATION

The media talks about issues that affect politics in a society.

The political parties adapt what they say and try to steer the conversation toward topics that they want to be included on the political agenda.

Political parties try to influence the vote.

Topics and opinions are broadcast through the media (television, radio, newspapers, internet, social media). People can listen to the different opinions on an issue and form their own opinion.

Although in fact, people tend to look for and listen to the opinions that are most similar to their own.

Finally, people give their support by voting for their chosen party.

!!
I believe
Let them come back

POPULISM

When we use the word "populism," we are talking about the speeches that some politicians make when they put forward simple solutions to complex problems. They use simple, aggressive, and direct language that everyone can understand and share.

Us

The enemy (the others)

They often claim that the people responsible for all the bad things in society are a "corrupt elite" who are acting against "us" (meaning the people, the nation, etc.). And they put forward (supposedly) radical measures to solve this.

Populism is very good at spreading its simple and effective messages through traditional media and on social media. This way, populists (who can be from the far left or the far right) manage to influence lots of people who end up voting for them.

In recent years, far-right populists have used identity politics (which is politics based on particular identities, such as race, nationality, or gender) to spread their aggressive messages, for example by stirring up a fear of migrants.

CORRUPTION

When there is a lot of political corruption in a country, we say it is a CORRUPT SYSTEM. By this we mean it is an inefficient state where most politicians and civil servants are working for their own personal benefit over and above their public responsibilities.

AN EXAMPLE OF CORRUPTION

A clear case of corruption would be a politician receiving money or gifts from a company in exchange for making political decisions that are favorable to the company, bypassing legal procedures and checks.

We talk about corruption when people illegally use public institutions for their own benefit and for financial, political, or professional gain.

PATRONAGE NETWORKS

These are people who form a group around a person with a lot of political or economic power and exchange favors, information, and loyalty.

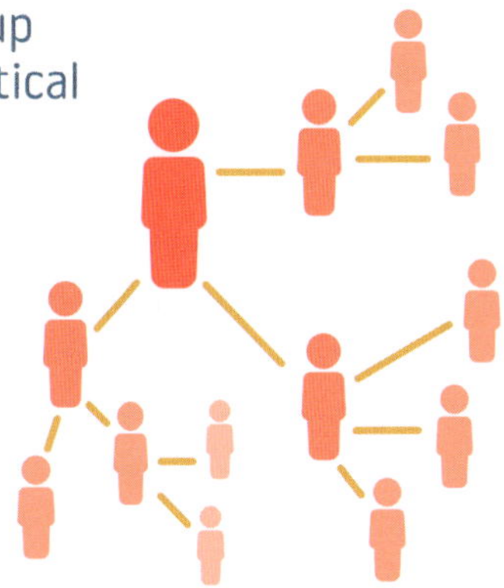

THE RICH WIN

Although laws are the same for everyone, if you are rich, you can hire the best experts and lawyers to defend your interests. You might even be able to bribe a corrupt judge or police officer.

Corruption damages democracy because it goes against the principles of the separation of powers and equality before the law.

Being a politician and governing is not an easy job. You often have to take decisions that some people like a lot and others don't like that much.

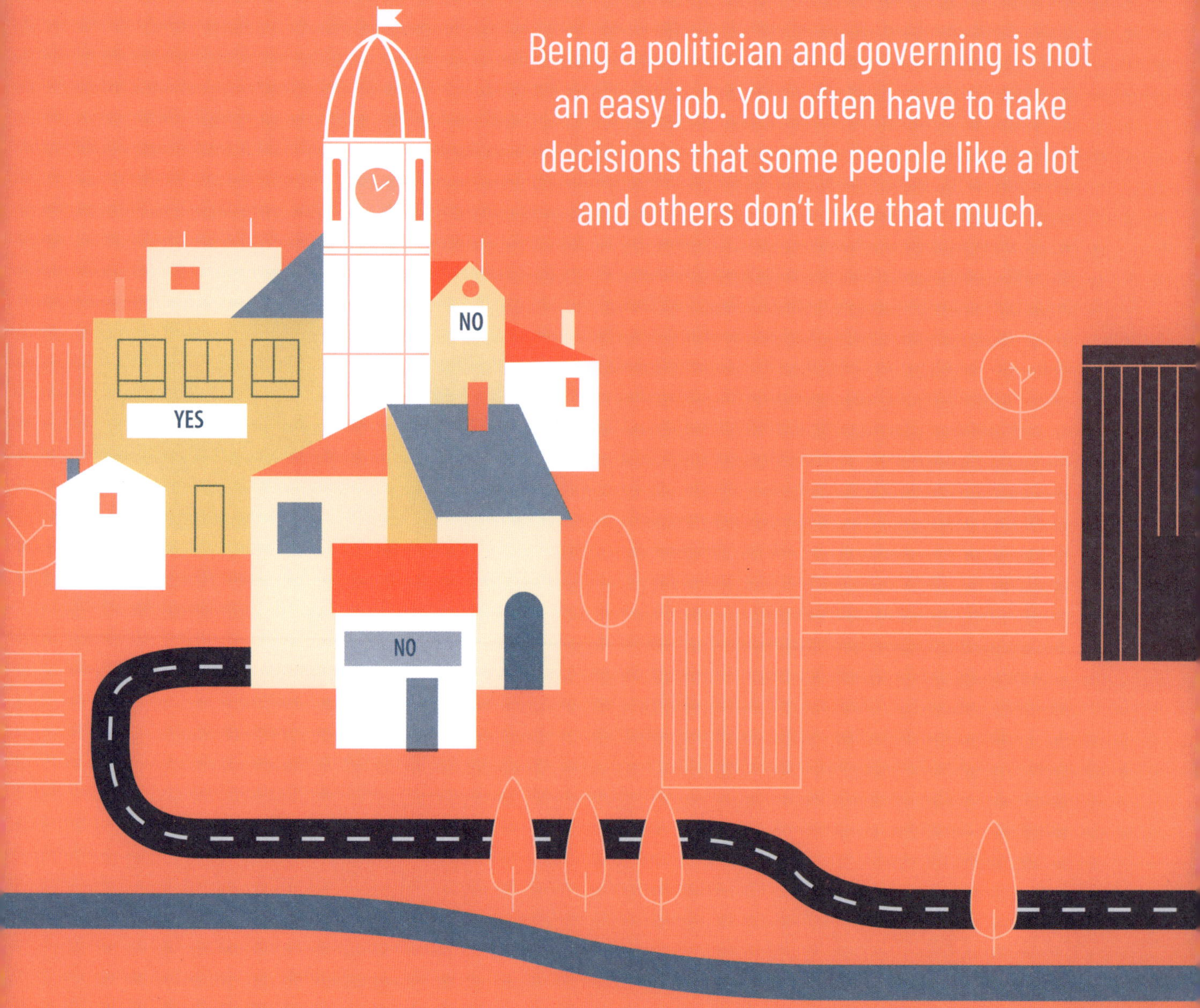

Environmental groups and lots of other people are against it because they think the factory will harm the environment and have a very negative impact on the landscape and the countryside around the town.

But many others are in favor of it because they think it will bring jobs to people in the town. Also, the taxes the company will pay to the town council would be used to improve lots of things.

The town council has to give permission to build the factory. And the local elections are coming up.

Imagine you are the mayor of a town. A big multinational company would like to build a factory on land close to the river.

What would you do?

What if I disagree?

In a democracy, people do not have the right to break laws, but they do have the right to make their voice heard and take action to change things.

RIGHT TO PROTEST—In democracies, everyone has the right to express their opinions, to meet with other people, and to protest, take action, demonstrate, use art, or whatever they want (as long as it is legal).

Social movements

In many cases, people come together and join organizations, associations, clubs, and NGOs* that fight for issues they care about.

Some of these groups might be created for a particular issue that affects a neighborhood or city. Others are organizations that focus on wider issues that a group of people are concerned about and want to take action on, for example, animal welfare, housing, medical research, the rights of migrants, women's rights, racism, and the problems affecting homeless people.

People who are very involved in a cause or a movement are called activists.

*Non-governmental organizations—nonprofit groups set up independently from governments.

The power of the people

People can bring about change if they unite. A demonstration—when people get together as a group to support or protest against a person or a cause—gets television and social media coverage and can influence public opinion and government decisions.

In fact, that is the purpose of many demonstrations: for people to publicly express their disagreement or support for an issue. And in most cases, the bigger the demonstration, the more impact it will have.

A demonstration may also end in disorder, riots, and confrontation with the police. Violence (although illegal) is also a means to get coverage and exert pressure.

And if the pressure of the masses is very strong, it can end up forcing political change and even lead to REVOLUTION or war.

GLOSSARY

Allegiance: loyalty to a leader, group, or idea.

Assembly: a group of people that gather together to find solutions for a common problem or to achieve a common goal.

Authoritarian(ism): in an authoritarian political system, power is concentrated in the hands of one leader or one government and people need to obey their will and decisions without questioning them.

Broadcast: to send out a message or program on television or radio or over the internet.

Candidate: someone who is being considered for a position—for example, someone who is running for the position of prime minister or president of a country.

Censorship: to control what can be read, heard, or seen.

Ceremonial: a set of formal actions that take place on formal occasions.

Customs official (or customs officer): someone who checks travellers' luggage to make sure that they are not taking goods into a country that are not allowed without paying taxes.

Diversity: recognizing, respecting, and valuing the differences among people, including age, gender, physical and mental ability, race, and religion.

Empire: a large territory made up of many states and ruled by an emperor.

Entity(ies): something that exists independently. It can be a person, partnership, organization, or company.

Equality: providing the same opportunities to everyone and making sure that people are not discriminated against because of their differences.

Executive (government): the branch of the government that is responsible for making sure that laws, policies, and decisions are put into action.

Feudal(ism): a society that is based around ownership of land in exchange for service of labor.

Government: a group of people that have the power or right to govern (rule) a country.

Identity politics: a set of ideas and actions that are driven by a particular identity, such as gender, class, race, religion, or nationality.

Ideology: a set of ideas about how society should be.

Immigration: the movement of a person or a group of people (immigrants) from one country to another to live there permanently.

Infrastructure: the structures and facilities that are needed for a society to function, such as buildings, roads, electrical grids, railways, telecommunication networks, etc.

Judicial/judiciary: the branch of the government that is responsible for a country's legal system.

Justice: fairness in the way people are dealt with.

Kingdom: a country that is ruled by a king or queen. A kingdom is smaller than an empire.

Labor union (or trade union): an organization that represents workers in a particular industry and seeks to improve their working conditions.

Legislative: the branch of the government that makes laws.

Majority: a number or percentage that is more than half of the total (for example, a party that receives 55% of the votes has the majority).

Manifesto: a written statement that sets out the aims, intentions, and beliefs of a person or group. The manifestos of political parties outline their aims and the policies they will put into place if they are elected.

Migration: the movement of an individual or a group of people (migrants) from one place to another to seek work or better living conditions. Migration can be someone's own choice (because they want to improve their life) or it can be forced due to war.

Nationalist: a person who believes their country is better than others, and who may also be hostile toward immigrants coming to their country.

Open forum: a place where people meet to exchange ideas and discuss public matters.

Organization: a group of people that work together towards a common goal.

Political conflict: a disagreement between groups or individuals who have different views and goals.

Polls: surveys that collect people's opinions on different topics.

President: the head of state in presidential systems.

Prestige: if a person or thing has prestige, it means they are respected and admired. This might be because of their success, wealth, or position in society.

Prime minister: the leader of the government in a country that has a parliamentary system.

Private property: land or anything a person owns that no one else can use without their permission.

Regime: a system of government.

Regulate: to control something according to rules.

Regulations: rules made by the government to control (or *regulate*) something.

Representative: a person or a body of people that are chosen to act on behalf of a wider group. for example, a member of Congress in the USA, or a Member of Parliament (MP) in the UK.

Representative democracy: also known as electoral democracy, this is the most advanced type of democracy, where the people elect representatives to make policies and laws on their behalf.

Repression: the action of bringing people under control by using force.

Reprisal: an act of retaliation, for example an action or threat of action against someone that has done something wrong to you, your group, or your country.

Resources: everything in our environment that can be used to meet our needs. For example, natural resources such as oil, natural gas, stone, and sand can be used to construct buildings.

Revolution: an attempt by many people to rapidly change the way a society is organized by overthrowing a government or ruler and replacing them with a new one. Revolutions use methods such as protests, strikes, or violence, instead of voting.

Shareholders: someone who owns shares in a company. In return for investing money in the company, a shareholder is given a share of the ownership of the company.

Social class: groupings of people in society based on factors such as wealth, income, education, job, and family background. The most common categories are upper class, middle class, and working class.

Society: a group of people who live in a community in the same territory. The people in the society may share the same institutions and cultural ideas.

Sovereignty: the authority of a state to govern its territory. Sovereignty also refers to the highest power or authority—for example, in a monarchy, the king or queen has sovereignty (the highest power) over the country.

Supranational: having power and authority that goes above national borders or governments. For example, the World Trade Organization is a supranational organization that promotes international trade by making rules and agreements that are respected by all of the member states within the organization.

Trade union: *see* Labor union.

First published 2024 in English by Button Books, an imprint of Guild of Master Craftsman Publications Ltd, Castle Place, 166 High Street, Lewes, East Sussex, BN7 1XU, UK. Illustrations © Eduard Altarriba i Bigas, 2024. Text © Eduard Altarriba i Bigas and Meli, 2024. English text © GMC Publications Ltd, 2024. ISBN: 978-1-78708-151-2. Distributed by Publishers Group West in the United States. All rights reserved. This translation of *Politics* is published by arrangement with Asterisc Agents. The right of Eduard Altarriba to be identified as the author of this work has been asserted in accordance with the Copyright, Designs and Patents Act 1988, sections 77 and 78. No part of this publication may be reproduced, stored in a retrieval system, or transmitted in any form or by any means without the prior permission of the publisher and copyright owner. While every effort has been made to obtain permission from the copyright holders for all material used in this book, the publishers will be pleased to hear from anyone who has not been appropriately acknowledged and to make the correction in future reprints. The publishers and authors can accept no legal responsibility for any consequences arising from the application of information, advice, or instructions given in this publication. A catalog record for this book is available from the British Library. For Alababalà, Consultant: Marc Gallifa; Designer and Editor: Meli. For GMC Publications, Publisher: Jonathan Bailey; Production Director: Jim Bulley; Senior Project Editor: Tom Kitch; Design Manager: Robin Shields; English Translation: Andrea Reece; Editor: Claire Saunders; Editorial Advisor: Dr. Stavroula Chrona. Color origination by GMC Reprographics. Printed and bound in China.

Button Books

FSC
www.fsc.org
MIX
Paper | Supporting responsible forestry
FSC® C144853